LEVEL **1**

Leah Walker

THE REAL EASY BOOK
TUNES FOR BEGINNING IMPROVISERS

A Sher Music Co. Publication
Produced in conjunction with
the Stanford Jazz Workshop
www.stanfordjazz.org

Publisher - Chuck Sher
Conceived and Edited by - Michael Zisman
Educational Consultants - Bennett Paster, Ray Scott, James Nadel, Mark Levine
Music Copying, Layout and Editing - Chuck Gee, San Francisco, CA
Cover Design - Attila Nagy, Cotati, CA

©2003 Sher Music Co. • P.O. Box 445, Petaluma, CA 94953 • www.shermusic.com
ISBN 1-883217-19-9

i

Index Of Tunes

What Is Unique About This Book?

THE REAL EASY BOOK was originally developed at the Stanford Jazz Workshop for use in our beginning jazz combo classes. We needed a collection of jazz songs that sounded good, were easy to learn, fun to play, and open enough to accommodate the varied teaching approaches of our diverse faculty.

These compositions, written by well-known jazz artists, are great examples of basic jazz melody, phrasing, harmony, rhythm and form. Many beginning students have difficulties playing standards (like *Autumn Leaves*) in a jazz style because they lack the experience and interpretive skills required to do so. Since the compositions in this book were <u>written</u> as jazz tunes, they will sound like jazz the first time they are sight-read.

By playing these tunes and learning the basic material to be found in them, the student will develop his or her jazz sensibility and will then be able to apply it to any music. Additionally, due to the rhythmic strength and phrasing of the melodies, these songs will often sound good in many styles, including rock, funk, Latin, etc. In short, this book is ideal for students of all ages and backgrounds.

THE REAL EASY BOOK is <u>not</u> intended to be a method book. Instead, we have combined clear lead-sheets with basic educational material that any student, teacher or band director will find helpful.
- ◆Individual students can study alone or use this book in conjunction with private instruction.
- ◆Jazz teachers can use this book as a vehicle to teach their lessons to beginning jazz students and combos.
- ◆Band directors with beginning combos can use this book as a starting point for developing repertoire and arrangements.

Supplementary educational material, including scales, chord voicings and bass lines, appear in all four transpositions of this book so that students on all instruments can better understand the roles of the other players in the ensemble. There is also an appendix of more reference material at the end of the book.

Since many of the songs in this collection are part of the standard jazz repertoire, students can play them at jam sessions or even at gigs! We hope THE REAL EASY BOOK brings you many happy hours learning to play one of the greatest art forms ever created - jazz music!

PLEASE NOTE:
Unlike Sher Music Co.'s other jazz fake books, these lead sheets are **not transcriptions** from particular recordings. Rather, they have been adapted (and sometimes simplified from the definitive version) so that the beginning jazz student can easily play them and gain a clear understanding of basic jazz fundamentals. The definitive versions of many of these tunes can be found in *The New Real Books*, available at www.shermusic.com or at 800/444-7437.

How To Use This Book

PLEASE NOTE: In the Bb and Eb editions, all melody notes, chords and supplemental materials have been transposed into the appropriate keys.

The Songs: The charts in this book are basic lead-sheets, not arrangements. They do not include introductions, endings, comping rhythms, etc. Students and teachers are encouraged to use their imagination to arrange the songs as desired. Developing these skills are essential for the jazz musician.

For some songs, the chord changes have been simplified in order to make the basic harmonic movement clear. Chords appear over the beat on which they should be played. Chords carry over to the next bar when no other chords appear. Some songs in this book have short forms; there are many 12-bar blues and 8 bar songs. It is common practice to repeat these melodies—both before and after solos.

The Supplemental Material: THE REAL EASY BOOK is <u>not</u> intended to be a method book. The supplemental material accompanying each tune is designed only to provide beginning jazz players quick access to the music, and to illustrate the fundamentals of harmony, voice leading, etc. There are many jazz method books that expand on these topics.

The Numbers: The Arabic numbers that are used beneath or next to notes in this book are provided for analytic purposes. They refer to scale degrees in relationship to the root of the current chord. Note that the numbers 2 and 9 refer to the same note name (as is true of 4 and 11, and also 6 and 13).

The Piano Voicings: There are two sets of basic piano chord voicings provided for study on each song. The first set, "Basic 3-Note Voicings", illustrates the root-motion and the resolution path of the 3rds and 7ths through the chord progression. Start with these voicings to understand the harmony of each song. For these voicings, play the treble clef notes in the right hand; play the bass clef notes in the left hand. You can invert the 3rds and 7ths to create an additional set of voicings.

The second set, "Rootless Voicings", does not include the root of the chord. This is stylistically typical of modern jazz piano; it assumes that a bass player will be playing the roots. These voicings do contain the 3rds and 7ths plus one additional note. Play them in either hand, or divide the notes between both hands. Notice how they connect smoothly to each other, with efficient hand motion. These voicings are useful for a pianist to accompany their own improvisation.

In some cases, there are notes in these chord voicings that are not written in the corresponding chord symbols. It is typical for a jazz piano player to add upper extensions (9ths, 11ths and 13ths) to chords, even when they are not specifically called for. These upper extensions have been added to chords where they are stylistically or harmonically appropriate.

The Scales: The use of scales is one of many ways to approach improvisation. We have provided one or more scales relating to the harmony of each song as a starting place. In parentheses after the scale name is the corresponding chord that the scale complements. Some scales (such as the blues scale) are included for general use on the tune. The student should explore the sound of these scales—and the many other scale possibilities—on their own and/or with a teacher.

The Bass Lines: One chorus of a sample bass line is provided to give the bass student an initial idea about how to approach each of these songs. For horn players using these lines, some of the notes in these bass lines may be below your range; it those cases feel free to take them up an octave. These bass lines may not be relevant if the style of the tune is changed from the original.

The Blank Staves have been included, where space permitted, for the student to take notes, to compose melodic ideas, to notate alternative scales, or to add other information.

The Drum Parts: Basic drum patterns for several styles are included in Appendix I at the back of the book. The songs in this book will generally work with these patterns or with others that the student may already know.

Study Hints:
- Try to memorize the music and the educational material. By digesting this information you will be able to use it freely in improvisation.
- Look for connections between the songs. Finding similarities will make them easier to learn.
- Don't be limited by the supplemental material presented with each song. Experiment and try new things. Asking instructors and fellow musicians questions is a great way to learn.
- Listen to recordings of the songs to see how other musicians have played them. See Appendix II - Discography for the most well-known versions of the songs.
- Play these songs in different styles. Try creating several different arrangements of each song. Imagination and creativity are essential to jazz.

Some Important Definitions

Form: It is common to label the different sections of a song with letters. If a song form is notated AABA, it has two different sections. The first section, A, is played twice, followed by B, commonly referred to as the "bridge", followed again by a restatement of A. There are many different variations of forms, such as ABA, AAB, ABAC, etc. Another common form in jazz is the 12-bar blues. In this book, the term "Blues" indicates a 12-bar form and is not meant to infer style.

Rhythmic Feels: All of the songs in this book will sound good played in different rhythmic feels, but on the charts we have roughly notated the feels in which the songs were originally played. We have consolidated these into three general categories: *swing, jazz waltz,* and *straight-eighth.*
- *Swing:* In this rhythmic feel, any two eighth notes on one beat are generally not played with equal value. Rather, they should be played as an eighth note triplet, with the first two notes in the triplet tied together.
- *Jazz Waltz:* This is the same as the swing feel, but in 3/4 meter.
- *Straight-Eighth:* Eighth notes should be played evenly. Most Latin, rock and funk styles have straight-eighth note feels.

Tempo: In most cases, we have indicated the general tempo at which the song was originally played. Here are some general metronomic guidelines.
Slow: quarter note = 80-120 beats per minute (bpm)
Medium: quarter note = 120-180 bpm
Fast: quarter note = 180 bpm, and above

About the Stanford Jazz Workshop

Founded in 1972, the Stanford Jazz Workshop (SJW) is a nonprofit organization dedicated to the perpetuation of jazz through educational programs and concerts of the highest artistic quality. Its mission is to create an environment conducive to learning, experiencing and appreciating jazz by assembling a community of the best performers and teachers of jazz, as well as students of all abilities and backgrounds.

Based in the San Francisco Bay Area, SJW produces internationally respected jazz education programs (including the Evening Summer Program, Jazz Camp, Jazz Residency and the Jazz Weekend Intensive) for adults, emerging professionals, young musicians and jazz educators. These programs have brought such legendary artists as Stan Getz, Dizzy Gillespie, McCoy Tyner, Horace Silver, Phil Woods, Hank Jones and Ray Brown to SJW to share their art and insight with new generations of jazz players. Among the thousands of students who have participated are musicians who are emerging as new stars of jazz, including Josh Redman, Larry Grenadier, Bill Stewart, Sylvia Cuenca and Taylor Eigsti.

SJW presents the annual Stanford Jazz Festival to coincide with its educational summer programs, in addition to year-round concert and masterclass events. As a presenter, SJW is distinguished by its commitment to providing audiences with entertaining performances that offer an historical and multicultural perspective on jazz in its entirety, and a tradition of presenting jazz masters, emerging talents, and unique premiere events. The overall experience of SJW's programs has been described by the *San Francisco Chronicle* as "Jazz Heaven."

SJW appreciates the contributions Sher Music Co. has made to jazz education by providing accurate and understandable charts for the professional jazz musician and student alike. Sher Music Co.'s many books have been important instructional resources for SJW student combos, theory classes and jam sessions. We are thrilled to join forces with Sher Music Co. to bring you this landmark publication, THE REAL EASY BOOK!

Editor's Notes

I would like to extend special thanks to:
- Bennett Paster, Ray Scott, Jim Nadel, Mark Levine, Bert Carelli, Carma Berglund and Alex
  Kharmats for all their expertise, hard work and understanding.
- Chuck Sher for helping me realize this project.
- Chuck Gee for his intelligent and helpful copying skills and great attitude.
- Gregory Ryan, John McKenna and Dena DeRose for their work on the original "Cookbook" project.
- Bob Parlocha for his sage advise and vast jazz library; Matt Clark, Larry Dunlap, Brad Buethe and
  Andrew Speight for their proofreading and other help; and David Rokeach for the drum appendix.
- The staff, faculty and students of the SJW for many great years of learning and playing.
- The great artists who wrote these tunes and inspire us all.

This book is dedicated to Jim Nadel on the 30th Anniversary of the Stanford Jazz Workshop.

Michael Zisman, Editor
1/1/03

The Tunes

RAY BROWN, OSCAR PETERSON & HERB ELLIS
Photo©Paul Hoeffler, Toronto, Canada

Bags' Groove

Milt Jackson

Bags' Groove is a 12-bar blues with a repeating motific melody that doesn't change to match the chords. This was originally played as a medium-slow swing.

For your use

Supplemental Material - Bags' Groove

Sample Piano Voicings

Basic 3-note voicings

Rootless voicings

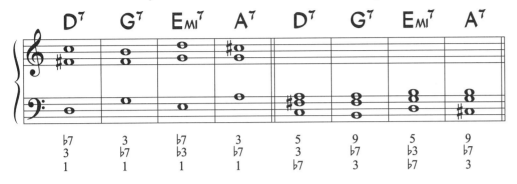

Useful Scales

D Blues Scale

Sample Bass Line

Big Bertha

Duke Pearson

Big Bertha has an AABA form. The rests in the A section melody leave spaces for the rhythm section to fill. This was originally played with a medium swing feel.

For your use

Supplemental Material - Big Bertha

Sample Piano Voicings

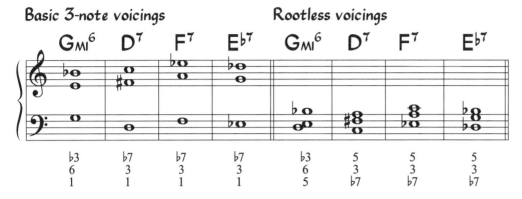

Useful Scales

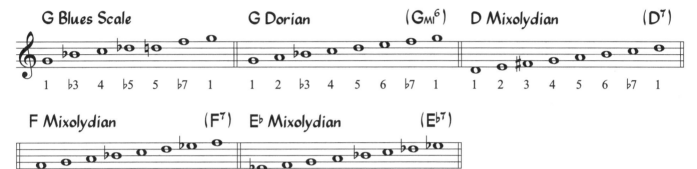

Sample Bass Line

5

Blue Seven

Sonny Rollins

©1965 Prestige Music Co. Used by Permission.

Blue Seven is a 12-bar blues that features a call and response melody.
Note the use of the ♭5 (also called the ♯11) in the melody over each of the three seventh chords.
This was originally played as a medium-slow swing.

For your use

Supplemental Material - Blue Seven

Sample Piano Voicings

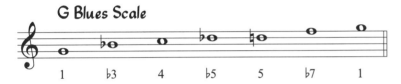

Useful Scales

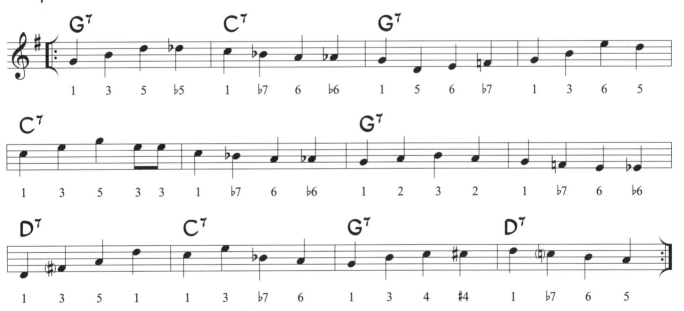

Sample Bass Line

Blues By Five

Red Garland

Blues By Five is a 12-bar blues where sections of the motific melody are transposed to match the chord changes. This was originally played with a medium-swing feel.

For your use

Supplemental Material - Blues By Five

Sample Piano Voicings

Basic 3-note voicings   Rootless voicings

G⁷	C⁷	D⁷	G⁷	C⁷	D⁷
3	♭7	♭7	9	13	5
♭7	3	3	♭7	3	3
1	1	1	3	♭7	♭7

Useful Scales

G Blues Scale

1	♭3	4	♭5	5	♭7	1

Sample Bass Line

G⁷
1 3 4 #4 5 4 3 2 1 5 6 ♭7 1 3 6 5

C⁷
1 3 5 3 3 1 ♭7 6 ♭6 1 2 3 2 1 ♭7 6 ♭6
                                    G⁷

D⁷
1 3 5 1 ♭7 6 5 ♭5 1 3 4 #4 1 ♭7 6 5
                        G⁷   D⁷

9

Blues In The Closet

Oscar Pettiford

Blues in the Closet is a 12-bar blues with a motific melody. One melody note gets changed in measure 5 so that the melody matches the chord changes. This was originally played with a medium-slow swing feel.

For your use

Supplemental Material - Blues In The Closet

Sample Piano Voicings

Basic 3-note voicings   Rootless voicings

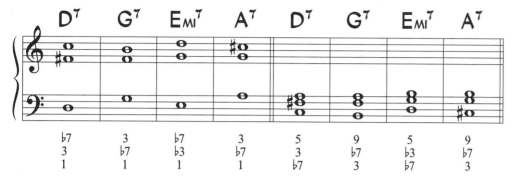

Useful Scales

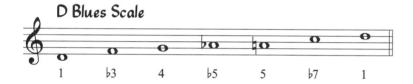

Sample Bass Line

Cold Duck Time

Eddie Harris

Cold Duck Time has a 12-bar form, but it does not use the typical 12-bar blues chord progression. It was originally played with a straight-eighth feel.

For your use

Supplemental Material - Cold Duck Time

Sample Piano Voicings

Basic 3-note voicings   Rootless voicings

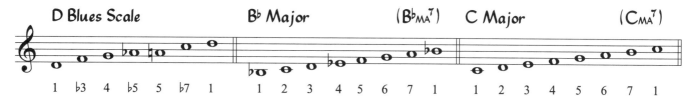

D⁷	G⁷	B♭ᴍᴀ⁷	Cᴍᴀ⁷	D⁷	G⁷	B♭ᴍᴀ⁷	Cᴍᴀ⁷
♭7	3	3	3	5	9	7	7
3	♭7	7	7	3	♭7	5	5
1	1	1	1	♭7	3	3	3

Useful Scales

D Blues Scale: 1 ♭3 4 ♭5 5 ♭7 1

B♭ Major (B♭ᴍᴀ⁷): 1 2 3 4 5 6 7 1

C Major (Cᴍᴀ⁷): 1 2 3 4 5 6 7 1

Sample Bass Line

D⁷ 1 5 1 5 ♭7 1   G⁷ 1 1 ♭7   D⁷ 1 5 1 5 ♭7 1   G⁷ 1 1 ♭7

B♭ᴍᴀ⁷ 1 1 1 1   Cᴍᴀ⁷ 1 1 1   D⁷ 1 1 1 1 1 5 ♭7 1

Contemplation

McCoy Tyner

Contemplation has a 16-bar form. The melodic phrases each end differently to match the chord changes. It was originally played with a slow jazz-waltz feel.

For your use

Supplemental Material - Contemplation

Sample Piano Voicings

Basic 3-note voicings   Rootless voicings

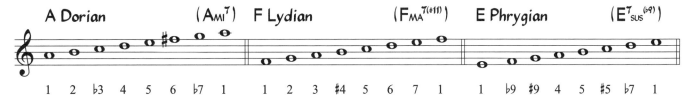

♭3	7	♭7	9	#4	5
♭7	3	4	♭7	3	4
1	1	1	♭3	7	♭7

Useful Scales

A Dorian   (A Mi⁷)   F Lydian   (F Ma⁷⁽#¹¹⁾)   E Phrygian   (E⁷ Sus ⁽♭⁹⁾)

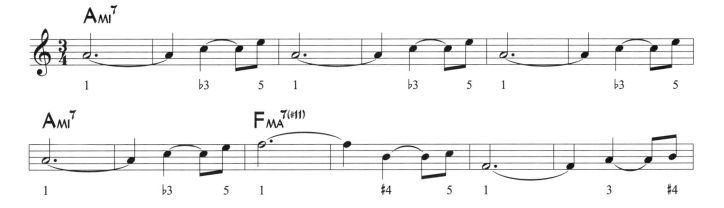

A Dorian: 1 2 ♭3 4 5 6 ♭7 1
F Lydian: 1 2 3 #4 5 6 7 1
E Phrygian: 1 ♭9 #9 4 5 #5 ♭7 1

Sample Bass Line

A Mi⁷
1   ♭3   5   1   ♭3   5   1   ♭3   5

A Mi⁷   F Ma⁷⁽#¹¹⁾
1   ♭3   5   1   #4   5   1   3   #4

E⁷ Sus ⁽♭⁹⁾
1   ♭2   4   1   ♭2   4

Doxy

Sonny Rollins

Doxy has a 16-bar form. It was originally played with a medium-slow swing feel.

For your use

Supplemental Material - Doxy

Sample Piano Voicings

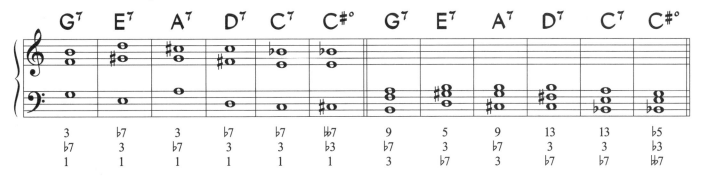

Useful Scales

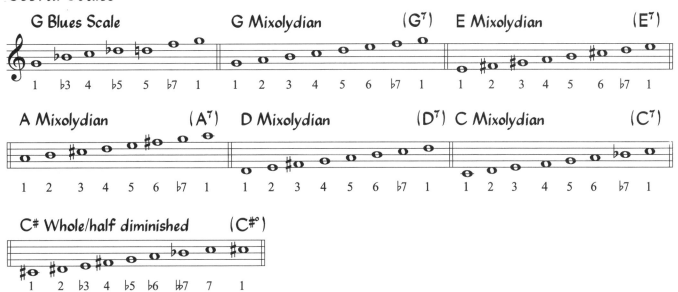

Sample Bass Line

Edward Lee

Harold Mabern, Jr.

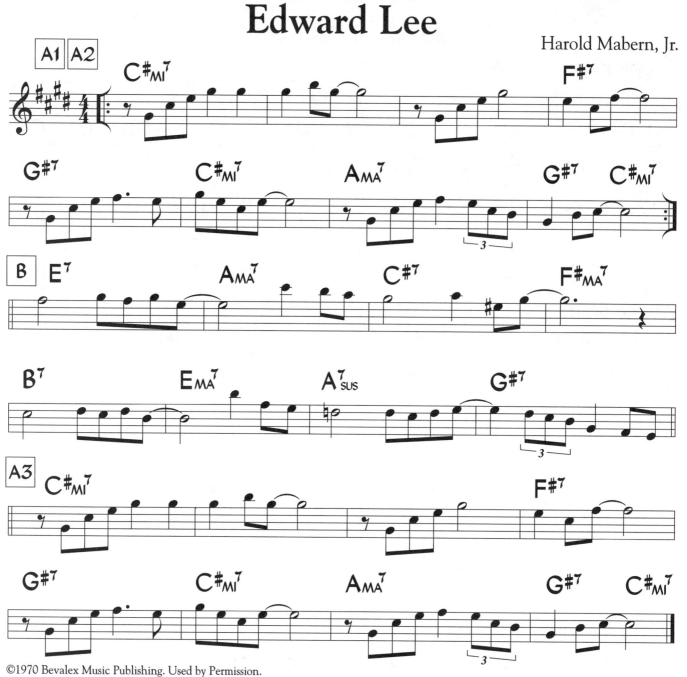

Edward Lee was originally played with a medium-swing feel.

For your use

Supplemental Material - Edward Lee

Sample Piano Voicings

Basic 3-note voicings

Rootless voicings

Useful Scales

Sample Bass Line

Equinox

John Coltrane

Equinox is a 12-bar minor blues. It was originally played with a slow swing feel.

For your use

Supplemental Material - Equinox

Sample Piano Voicings

Basic 3-note voicings   Rootless voicings

AMI⁷   DMI⁷   F⁷   E⁷   AMI⁷   DMI⁷   F⁷   E⁷

♭3	♭7	♭7	♭7	9	5	5	#5
♭7	♭3	3	3	♭7	♭3	3	3
1	1	1	1	♭3	♭7	♭7	♭7

Useful Scales

A Dorian   (AMI⁷)   A Blues Scale   F Mixolydian   (F⁷)   E Mixolydian   (E⁷)

1 2 ♭3 4 5 6 ♭7 1   1 ♭3 4 ♭5 5 ♭7 1   1 2 3 4 5 6 ♭7 1   1 2 3 4 5 6 ♭7 1

Sample Bass Lines

(Head) AMI⁷   DMI⁷

1   1   1   5 ♭7 1   1   1   1 ♭3 1   1   1   2   4

AMI⁷   F⁷   E⁷   AMI⁷

1   1   1   1   1   1   1   1   5 ♭7

(Solo) AMI⁷   DMI⁷

1 2 ♭3 4   5 6 ♭7 7   1 ♭7 5 ♭3   1 5 1 ♭3   1 2 ♭3 2   1 ♭7 6 ♭6

AMI⁷   F⁷   E⁷   AMI⁷

1 ♭7 6 ♭7   1 ♭3 5 ♭3   1 2 3 1   1 ♭7 ♭6 5   1 ♭3 5 ♭3   1 5 ♭3 2

Freedom Jazz Dance

Eddie Harris

Freedom Jazz Dance was originally played with a straight-eighth feel.

For your use

Supplemental Material - Freedom Jazz Dance

Sample Piano Voicings

Basic 3-note voicings   Rootless voicings

3	9	#9
b7	b7	b7
1	3	3

Useful Scales

G Blues Scale

| 1 | b3 | 4 | b5 | 5 | b7 | 1 |

Sample Bass Line

| 1 | | 5 | b7 | b7 | 5 | b7 | 1 | 1 | 1 | | 5 | b7 | b7 | 5 | b7 |

23

Gingerbread Boy

Jimmy Heath

Gingerbread Boy is a 16-bar modified blues. Solos are over a standard 12-bar blues progression. It was originally played with a medium-swing. In bars 11 and 12 the lower octave notes are the original melody.

(solo changes - 12-bar blues)

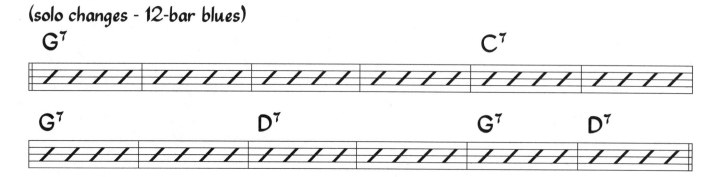

Supplemental Material - Gingerbread Boy

Sample Piano Voicings

Basic 3 and 4-note voicings

Rootless voicings

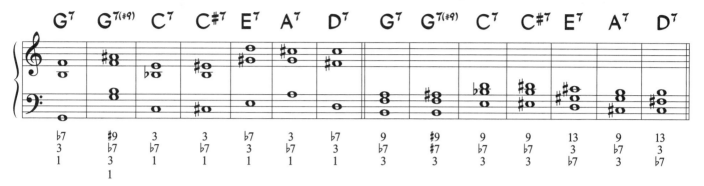

Useful Scales

G Blues Scale

Sample Bass Line

Groove Merchant

Jerome Richardson

Groove Merchant was originally played with a medium-swing feel.

For your use

Supplemental Material - Groove Merchant

Sample Piano Voicings

Basic 3-note voicings

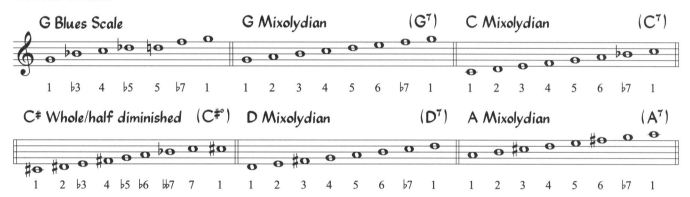

Rootless voicings

Useful scales

Sample Bass Line

Jive Samba

Nat Adderley

Jive Samba was originally played with a straight-eighth feel.

For your use

Supplemental Material - Jive Samba

Sample Piano Voicings

Basic 3-note voicings   Rootless voicings

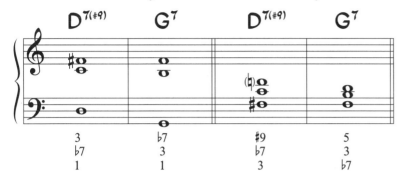

Useful Scales

Sample Bass Line For Solos

Jo Jo Calypso

Jim Nadel

Jo Jo Calypso was originally played with a straight-eighth feel.

For your use

Supplemental Material - Jo Jo Calypso

Sample Piano Voicings

Basic 3-note voicings   Rootless voicings

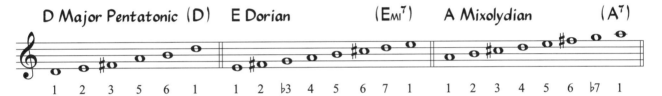

| | D | E_{MI}⁷ | A⁷ | D | E_{MI}⁷ | A⁷ |

Useful Scales

D Major Pentatonic (D)   E Dorian   (E_{MI}⁷)   A Mixolydian   (A⁷)

Sample Bass Line

D   E_{MI}⁷   A⁷   D   (etc.)

The Jody Grind

Horace Silver

The Jody Grind is a 12-bar blues with unusual harmony on the turnaround (the last 4 bars).
It was originally played with a straight-eighth feel.

For your use

Supplemental Material - The Jody Grind

Sample Piano Voicings

Basic 3-note voicings   Rootless voicings

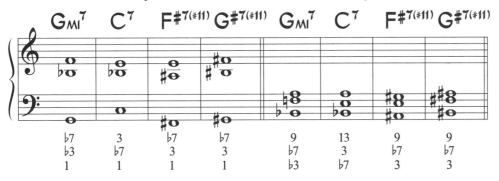

Useful Scales

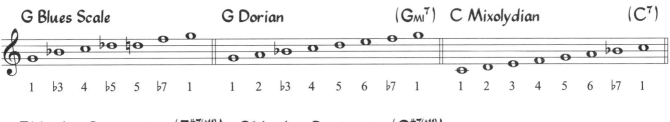

Sample Bass Line

33

Killer Joe

Benny Golson

Killer Joe has a 32-bar AABA form. The extreme contrast between the A and B sections creates a great sense of tension and release. It was originally played with a medium-swing feel.

Supplemental Material - Killer Joe

Sample Piano Voicings
Basic 3-note voicings

A7	G7	C#mi7(b5)	F#7(b9)	Cmi7	F7	F#7	F7	C#mi7	F#7
3	3	b3	b7	b3	b7	b7	b7	b3	b7
b7	b7	b7	3	b7	3	3	3	b7	3
1	1	1	1	1	1	1	1	1	1

Rootless voicings

A7	G7	C#mi7(b5)	F#7(b9)	Cmi7	F7	F#7	F7	C#mi7	F#7
9	9	b5	b9	5	9	9	9	9	9
b7	b7	b3	b3	b3	b7	b7	b7	b3	b7
3	3	b7	3	b7	3	3	3	b7	3

Useful Scales

A Blues Scale
| 1 | b3 | 4 | b5 | 5 | b7 | 1 |

A Mixolydian (A7)
| 1 | 2 | 3 | 4 | 5 | 6 | b7 | 1 |

G Mixolydian (G7)
| 1 | 2 | 3 | 4 | 5 | 6 | b7 | 1 |

F# Half/whole diminished (F#7(b9))
| 1 | b2 | b3 | 3 | b5 | b6 | bb7 | b7 | 1 |

F Mixolydian (F7)
| 1 | 2 | 3 | 4 | 5 | 6 | b7 | 1 |

F# Mixolydian (F#7)
| 1 | 2 | 3 | 4 | 5 | 6 | b7 | 1 |

Sample Bass Line

A1 A2 A7 G7 A7 G7 A7 G7
| 1 | 5 | 1 | 7 | 1 | 5 | 1 | #1 | 1 | 5 | 1 | 7 | 1 | 5 | 1 | #1 | 1 | 3 | 5 | 6 | 1 | b7 | 5 | 3 |

A7 G7 B C#mi7(b5) F#7(b9) Cmi7 F7
| 1 | 5 | 1 | 7 | 1 | 5 | 1 | #1 | 1 | b3 | b5 | b3 | 1 | b7 | 5 | 3 | 1 | 5 | 1 | b3 | 1 | 5 | 3 | 1 |

F#7 F7 C#mi7 F#7 A3 Play letter A
| 1 | 3 | 5 | 1 | 1 | 5 | 1 | 6 | 1 | b3 | 1 | 5 | 1 | 1 | 5 | 3 | 8 bars |

35

Listen Here

(2nd x, play 8va)

Eddie Harris

Listen Here was originally played with a straight-eighth feel.

For your use

Supplemental Material - Listen Here

Sample Piano Voicings

Basic 3-note voicings   Rootless voicings

Useful Scales

G Blues Scale

Sample Piano & Bass

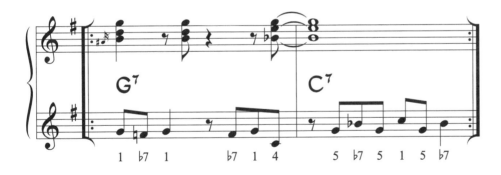

Little Sunflower

Freddie Hubbard

Little Sunflower was originally played with a straight-eighth feel.

For your use

Supplemental Material - Little Sunflower

Sample Piano Voicings

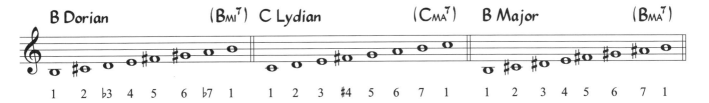

Useful Scales

Sample Bass Line

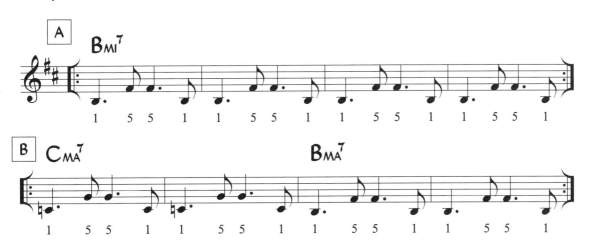

Mercy, Mercy, Mercy

Josef Zawinul

Mercy, Mercy, Mercy was originally played with a slow straight-eighth feel.

Supplemental Material - Mercy, Mercy, Mercy

Sample Piano Voicings

Basic 3-note voicings

G7	C7	G	C	D	D7sus	Ami7	Bmi7	Emi
♭7	3	5	3	3	♭7	♭3	♭3	5
3	♭7	3	5	5	4	♭7	♭7	♭3
1	1	1	1	1	1	1	1	1

Root and rootless voicings

G7	C7	G	C	D	D7sus	Ami7	Bmi7	Emi
9	13	1	5	5	5	1	1	5
♭7	3	5	3	3	4	♭7	♭7	♭3
3	♭7	3	1	1	♭7	♭3	♭3	1

Useful Scales

G Blues Scale   A Dorian   (Ami7)   B Dorian   (Bmi7)   E Aeolian   (Emi)

1 ♭3 4 ♭5 5 ♭7 1   1 2 ♭3 4 5 6 ♭7 1   1 2 ♭3 4 5 6 ♭7 1   1 2 ♭3 4 5 ♭6 ♭7 1

Sample Bass Line

Midnight Waltz

Cedar Walton

Midnight Waltz is a 24-bar blues that explores the tension and resolution between suspended 7th and dominant 7th chords. The A^7sus and D^7sus chords can all be played as straight dominant chords for the solos. This song was originally played with a jazz-waltz feel.

For your use

Supplemental Material - Midnight Waltz

Sample Piano Voicings

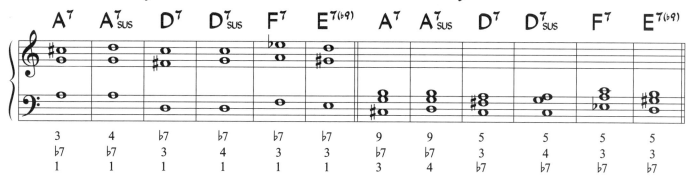

Useful Scales

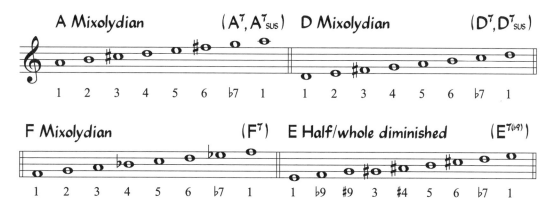

Sample Bass Line

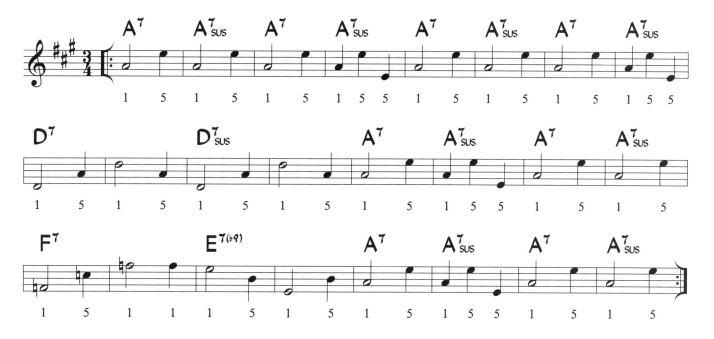

Mr. P.C.

John Coltrane

Mr. PC is a 12-bar minor blues. Segments of the motific melody are transposed to match the chord changes. It was originally played with a fast swing feel.

For your use

Supplemental Material - Mr. P.C.

Sample Piano Voicings

Basic 3-note voicings   Rootless voicings

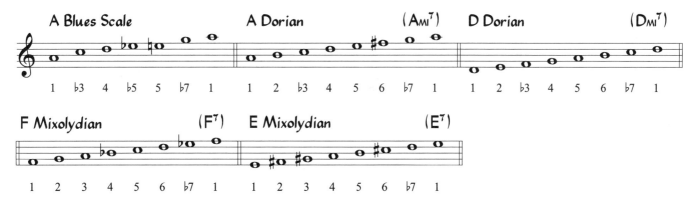

Useful Scales

Sample Bass Line

One For Daddy-O

Nat Adderley

One for Daddy-O is a 12-bar minor blues. This was originally played with a medium-slow swing feel. On the head, no chord is played on bars 5 and 6. Alternatively, use $G^{7(\#9)}$ instead of G_{MI}^{7} and $C^{7(\#9)}$ instead of the C_{MI}^{7} chord, on the head only.

For your use

Supplemental Material - One For Daddy-O

Sample Piano Voicings

Basic 3-note voicings   **Rootless voicings**

Useful Scales

Sample Bass Line

Red's Good Groove

Red Garland

Red's Good Groove is a 12-bar blues. It was originally played with a slow swing feel.

For your use

Supplemental Material - Red's Good Groove

Sample Piano Voicings

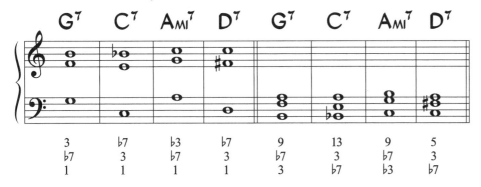

Useful Scales

Sample Bass Line

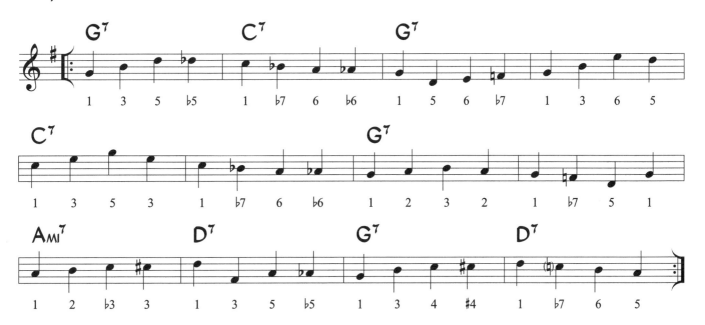

49

Revelation

Kenny Barron

Revelation is a 12-bar minor blues with a motivic melody. It was originally played with a medium-swing feel.

For your use

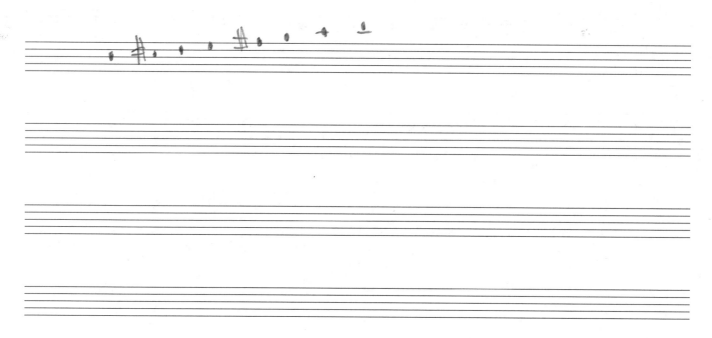

Supplemental Material - Revelation

Sample Piano Voicings

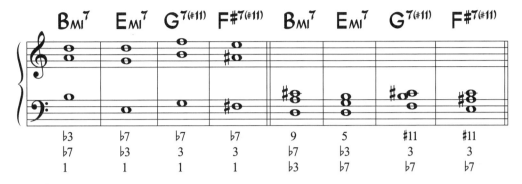

Useful Scales

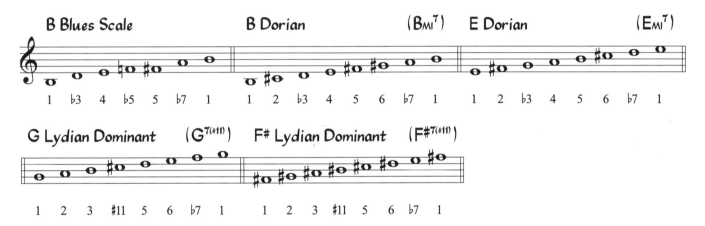

Sample Bass Line

51

Road Song

John L. ("Wes") Montgomery

Road Song has a 32-bar, AABA form. It was originally played with a straight-eighth feel.
For solos, disregard the $B^{7(\#9)}$ in bar 8 of each A section.

For your use

Supplemental Material - Road Song

Sample Piano Voicings

Useful Scales

Sample Bass Line

Short Stuff

Cedar Walton

Short Stuff has an 8-bar form with a descending turnaround. It was originally played with a medium-slow swing feel.

For your use

Supplemental Material - Short Stuff

Sample Piano Voicings

Basic 3-note voicings   **Rootless voicings**

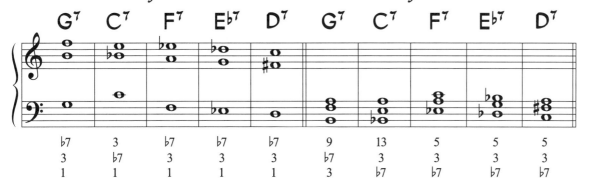

Useful Scales

Sample Bass Line

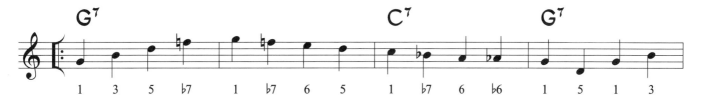

Shoshana

Piano Montuno

Mark Levine

Shoshana features a rhythmic piano part called a "montuno." Other instruments can play this for
arrangement purposes. This song was originally played with a straight-eighth feel. Solos are over
the A section only. The B section is written to be an interlude. It is a single-line melody; lower octave
has been provided in case the higher notes are above your range.

Supplemental Material - Shoshana

Sample Piano Voicings

Useful scales

Sample Bass Line

57

Sir John
(C⁷)

Blue Mitchell

Sir John is a 12-bar blues. It was originally played with a medium-swing feel.
The C⁶ chord in bar 2 should be played as C⁷ during solos.

For your use

Supplemental Material - Sir John

Sample Piano Voicings

Useful Scales

Sample Bass Line

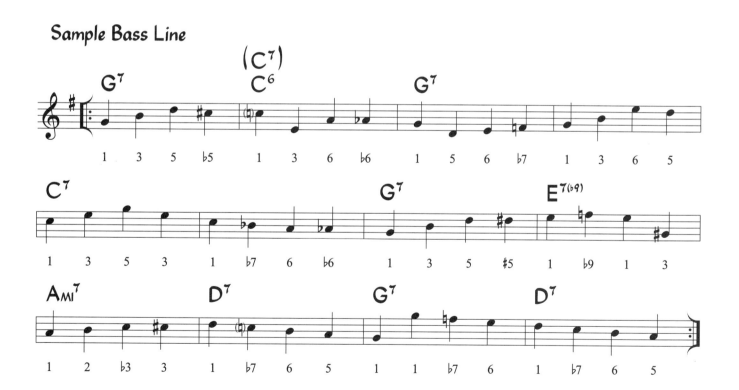

Sister Sadie

Horace Silver

Sister Sadie has a 32-bar, AABA form. The melody is accompanied by stop-time hits from the rhythm section. It was originally recorded with a medium-swing feel.

Supplemental Material - Sister Sadie

Sample Piano Voicings

Basic 3-note voicings

Rootless voicings

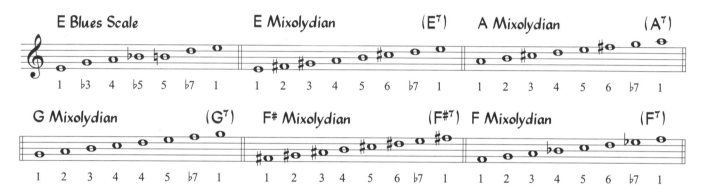

	E⁷	F⁷	A⁷	G⁷	F#⁷	F⁷	E⁷	F⁷	A⁷	G⁷	F#⁷	F⁷
	3	3	♭7	♭7	♭7	♭7	13	5	9	9	9	9
	♭7	♭7	3	3	3	3	3	3	♭7	♭7	♭7	♭7
	1	1	1	1	1	1	♭7	♭7	3	3	3	3

Useful Scales

E Blues Scale

1 ♭3 4 ♭5 5 ♭7 1

E Mixolydian (E⁷)

1 2 3 4 5 6 ♭7 1

A Mixolydian (A⁷)

1 2 3 4 5 6 ♭7 1

G Mixolydian (G⁷)

1 2 3 4 5 ♭7 1

F# Mixolydian (F#⁷)

1 2 3 4 5 6 ♭7 1

F Mixolydian (F⁷)

1 2 3 4 5 6 ♭7 1

Sample Bass Line

A1 A2 E⁷

1 2 3 4 5 6 ♭7 6 5 4 3 4 5 6 ♭7 7 1 6 5 4 3 6 5 ♭7

E⁷　　　　　　　B A⁷　　　　　E⁷

1 7 ♭7 6 5 4 2 2 1 3 5 6 ♭7 5 3 1 2 3 2 1 ♭7 6 5

A⁷　　G⁷　　F#⁷　　F⁷　　A3 Play letter A

1 3 5 3 1 3 5 3 1 3 5 3 1 3 5 ♭7 1 5 3 1　8 bars

Só Danço Samba

Music by
Antonio Carlos Jobim

Só Danço Samba is a 32-bar tune with an AABA form. It has a similar chord progression to Billy Strayhorn's Take The A Train. This song was originally played with a straight-eighth feel.

Supplemental Material - Só Danço Samba

Sample Piano Voicings

Basic 3-note voicings   Rootless voicings

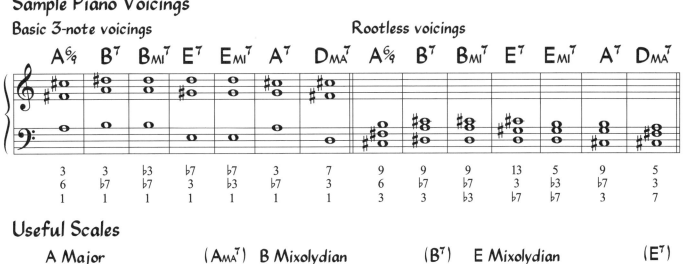

Useful Scales

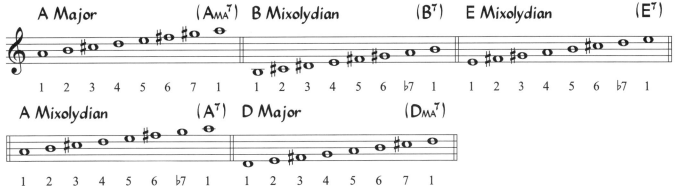

Sample Bass Lines

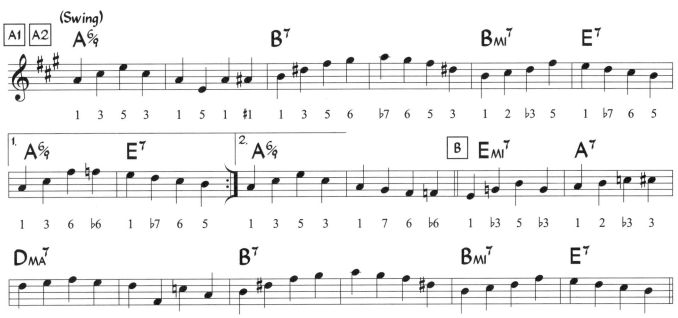

Song For My Father

Horace Silver

Song for My Father has an AAB form. It is common for the pianist to double the bass line during the melody. It was originally played with a straight-eighth feel.

Supplemental Material - Song For My Father

Sample Piano Voicings

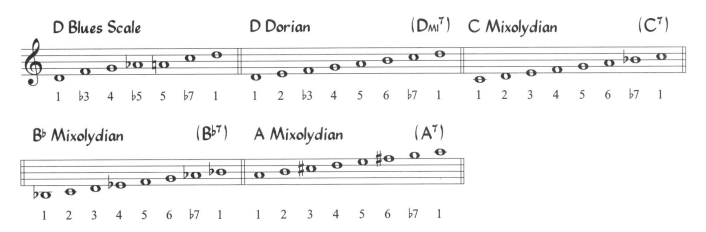

Useful Scales

Sonnymoon For Two

Sonny Rollins

Sonnymoon For Two is a 12-bar blues with a repeating motific melody that doesn't change to match the chords. This was originally played with a medium-swing feel.

For your use

Supplemental Material - Sonnymoon For Two

Sample Piano Voicings

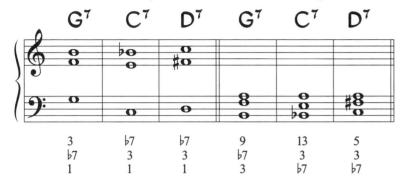

Basic 3-note voicings   Rootless voicings

G7	C7	D7	G7	C7	D7
3	♭7	♭7	9	13	5
♭7	3	3	♭7	3	3
1	1	1	3	♭7	♭7

Useful Scales

G Blues Scale

1	♭3	4	♭5	5	♭7	1

Sample Bass Line

St. James Infirmary

Joe Primrose

Saint James Infirmary is usually played with a slow-swing feel.

For your use

Supplemental Material - St. James Infirmary

Sample Piano Voicings

Basic 3-note voicings

Rootless voicings

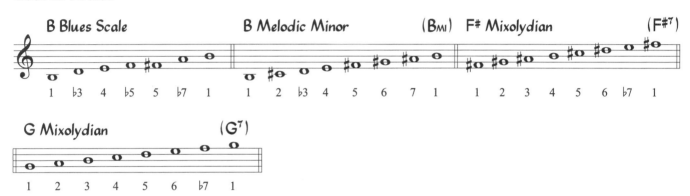

Useful Scales

Sample Bass Line

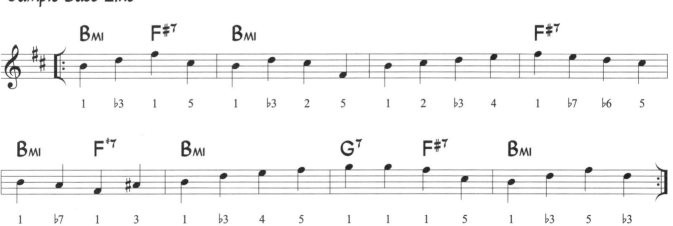

St. Thomas

Sonny Rollins

St. Thomas was originally played with a straight-eighth feel.

For your use

Supplemental Material - St. Thomas

Sample Piano Voicings

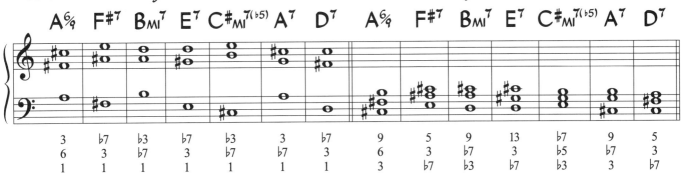

Useful Scales

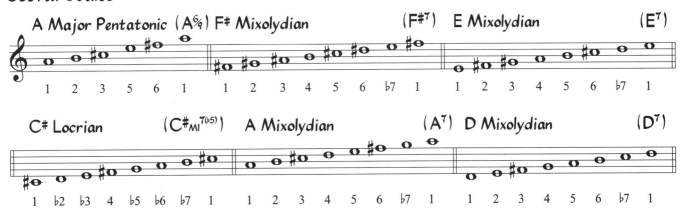

Sample Bass Line

Straight Life

Freddie Hubbard

Straight Life has a simple melody based on scales. It was originally played with a straight-eighth feel.

For your use

Supplemental Material - Straight Life

Sample Piano Voicings

Basic 3-note voicings   Rootless voicings

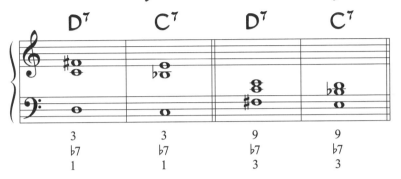

Useful Scales

D Blues Scale

Sample Bass Line

Tenor Madness

Sonny Rollins

Tenor Madness is 12-bar blues with a bebop melody. It was originally played with a medium-fast swing feel.

For your use

Supplemental Material - Tenor Madness

Sample Piano Voicings

Basic 3-note voicings   **Rootless voicings**

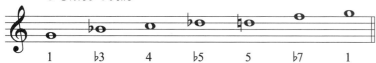

Useful Scales

G Blues Scale

Sample Bass Line

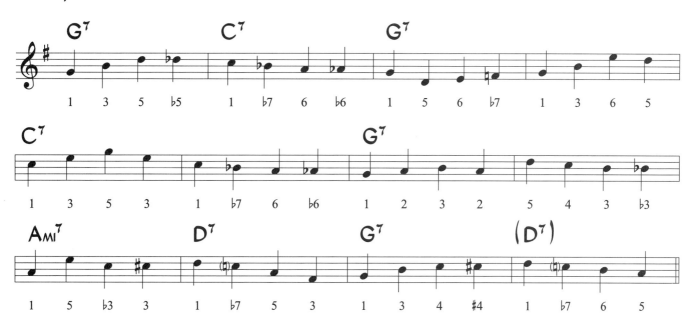

Trail Dust

Jim Rotondi

Trail Dust was originally played with a medium-swing feel.

For your use

Supplemental Material - Trail Dust

Sample Piano Voicings

Basic 3-note voicings

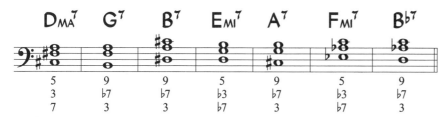

Rootless voicings

Useful Scales

Sample Bass Line

When The Saints Go Marching In

Traditional

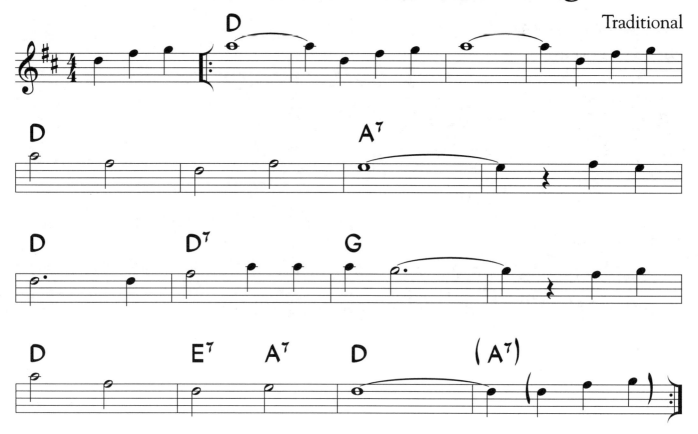

When The Saints Go Marching In is usually played with a medium-swing feel.

For your use

Supplemental Material - When The Saints Go Marching In

Sample Piano Voicings

Basic 3-note voicings

Root and rootless voicings

Useful Scales

Sample Bass Line

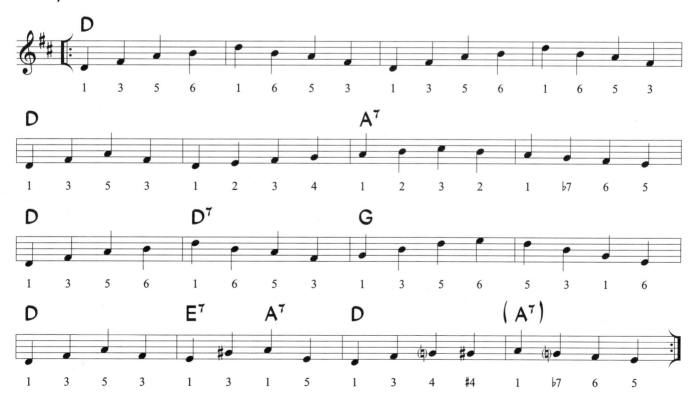

79

Work Song

Nat Adderley

Work Song has a 16 bar form and a call and response melody. It was originally played
with a medium swing feel.

Supplemental Material - Work Song

Sample Piano Voicings

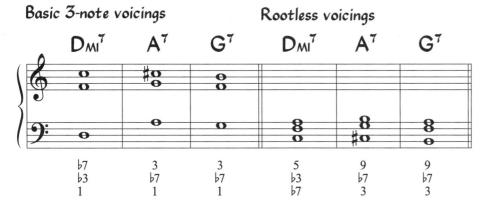

Useful Scales

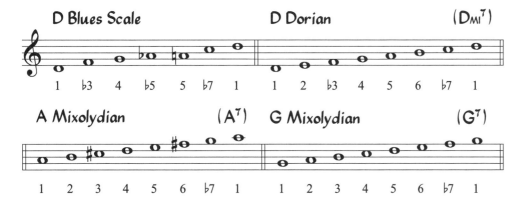

Sample Bass Line

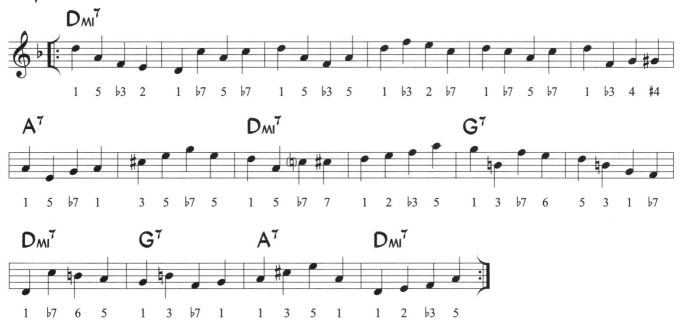

Yardbird Suite

Charlie Parker

Yardbird Suite has a 32-bar AABA form and a bebop melody. It was originally played with a medium-fast swing feel. The G^7 chords in parentheses are optional.

Supplemental Material - Yardbird Suite

Sample Piano Voicings

Basic 3-note voicings

Rootless voicings

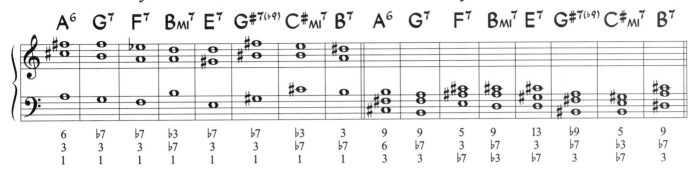

Useful scales

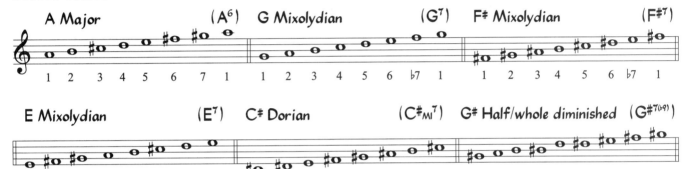

Sample Bass Line

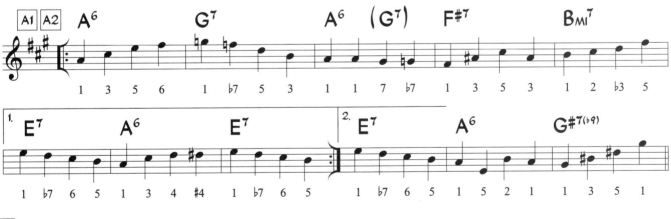

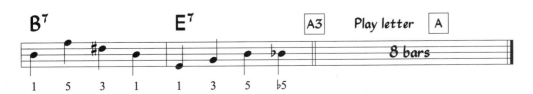

Z's Blues

Eric Alexander

Z's Blues is a 12-bar blues that was originally played with a medium-swing feel.

For your use

Supplemental Material - Z's Blues

Sample Piano Voicings

Basic 3-note voicings

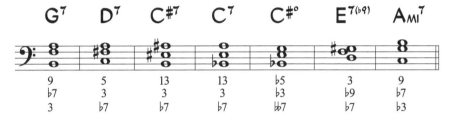

Root and rootless voicings

Useful Scales

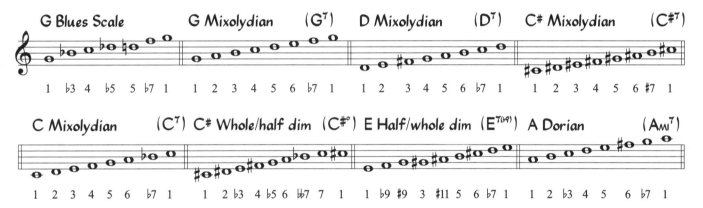

Sample Bass Line

Appendix I - Additional Educational Material

Chords and Complementary Scales

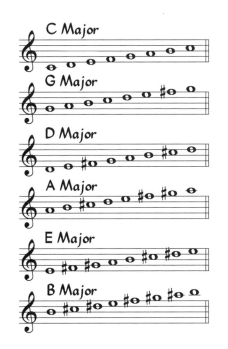
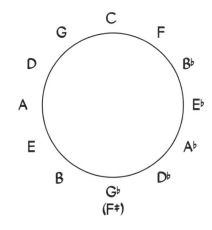
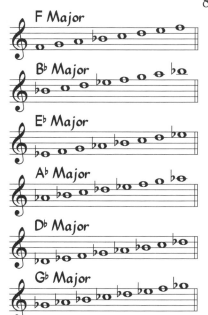

Cycle of Fifths

Move clockwise down a fifth,
move counterclockwise up a fifth.

Transposing A Riff

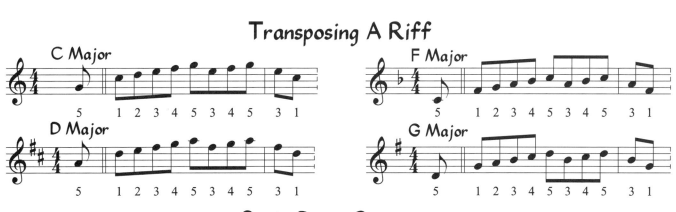

Basic Drum Patterns

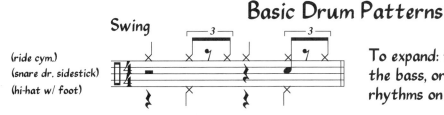

To expand: try playing light quarter notes on the bass, or try improvising different comping rhythms on the snare.

To expand: play the ride cymbal pattern on the (closed) hi-hat.

You can try varying the bass drum pattern, opening and closing the hi-hat, or playing the hi-hat pattern on the ride cymbal when appropriate.

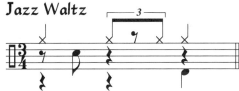

To expand: try playing light quarter notes on the bass, or try improvising different comping rhythms on the snare.

Appendix II - Discography

Below are the original &/or most well-known versions of the tunes in THE REAL EASY BOOK. You will definately benefit by listening to how the masters play this material!

1. Bags' Groove . . . . Miles Davis' "Bags' Groove"; MJQ's "Modern Jazz Quartet:1957"
2. Big Bertha . . . . Duke Pearson's "Sweet Honey Bee"
3. Blue Seven . . . . Sonny Rollins' "Saxophone Colossus"
4. Blues By Five . . . . Miles Davis' "Cookin' With The Miles Davis Quintet"
5. Blues In The Closet . . . . Bud Powell's "Blues In The Closet"
6. Cold Duck Time . . . . Les McCann & Eddie Harris' "Swiss Movement"
7. Contemplation . . . . McCoy Tyner's "The Real McCoy"
8. Doxy . . . . Miles Davis' "Bags' Groove"; "Sonny Rollins And The Big Brass"
9. Edward Lee . . . . "Eric Alexander Quartet Live At The Keynote"
10. Equinox . . . . .John Coltrane's "Coltrane's Sound"
11. Freedom Jazz Dance . . . . "The Best Of Eddie Harris"; Miles Davis' "Miles Smiles"
12. Gingerbread Boy . . . . Miles Davis' "Miles Smiles"; Jimmy Heath Quintet's "On The Trail"
13. Groove Merchant . . . . Jerome Richardson's "Jazz Station Runaway", Thad Jones/Mel Lewis
    Orchestra's "Basle 1969"
14. Jive Samba . . . . Cannonball Adderley's "Dizzy's Business"
15. Jo Jo Calypso . . . . .Not currently recorded
17. Killer Joe . . . . Art Farmer/Benny Golson & The Jazztet's "Meet The Jazztet"
18. Listen Here . . . . "The Best Of Eddie Harris"
19. Little Sunflower . . . . Freddie Hubbard's "Backlash"
20. Mercy, Mercy, Mercy . . . . Cannonball Adderley's "Mercy, Mercy, Mercy"
21. Midnight Waltz . . . . Cedar Walton's "Among Friends"
22. Mr. P.C . . . . John Coltrane's "Giant Steps"
23. One For Daddy-O . . . . Miles Davis' "Somethin' Else"
24. Red's Good Groove . . . . Red Garland's "Red's Good Groove"
25. Revelation . . . . .Yusef Lateef's "The Centaur And The Phoenix"
26. Road Song . . . . "Wes Montgomery's Finest Hour"
27. Short Stuff . . . . Cedar Walton's "Cedar!"
28. Shoshana . . . . Cal Tjader's "Both Sides Of The Coin"
29. Sir John . . . . Blue Mitchell's "Blue's Moods"
30. Sister Sadie . . . . Horace Silver's "Blowin' The Blues Away"
31. Só Danço Samba . . . . "Antonio Carlos Jobim: The Composer Of Desafinado, Plays";
    Stan Getz/João Gilberto's "Getz/Gilberto"
32. Song For My Father . . . . Horace Silver's "Song For My Father"
33. Sonnymoon For Two . . . . Sonny Rollins' "A Night At The Village Vanguard"
34. St. James Infirmary . . . . Louis Armstrong's "Satch Blows The Blues"
35. St. Thomas. Sonny Rollins' "Saxophone Colossus"
36. Straight Life . . . . Freddie Hubbard's "Straight Life"
37. Tenor Madness . . . . Sonny Rollins' "Tenor Madness"
38. Trail Dust . . . . Not currently recorded
39. When The Saints Go Marching In . . . . Louis Armstrong's "Golden Greats"
40. Work Song. . . . . .Cannonball Adderley's "Them Dirty Blues"
41. Yardbird Suite . . . . Charlie Parker's "The Savoy And Dial Master Takes"
42. Z's Blues . . . . Not currently recorded

STANFORD JAZZ WORKSHOP

Study and play with the best in jazz...
Programs for adults and youth

PAST FACULTY HAS INCLUDED:

Ray Brown	**Dizzy Gillespie**	**Sheila Jordan**
Regina Carter	**Joe Henderson**	**John Scofield**
Stan Getz	**Billy Higgins**	**Chucho Valdés**

PROGRAMS INCLUDE:

Evening Summer Program
Late June – late July
Weekday evening classes for
musicians and listeners

Jazz Camp
ages 12–17
Late July - early August

Jazz Residency
adult & under 18 by audition
First week of August

The Jazz Weekend Intensive
Second weekend in August
A mini-residency program

Stanford Jazz Festival
Late June - mid-August
34 Concerts showcasing the full
spectrum of jazz style

Second Sunday Jazz Series
October – May
Top jazz artists in concerts and
masterclasses

Photo: Sam Rivers at Jazz Residency 2001 by Scott Chernis

info: 650.736.0324 * www.stanfordjazz.org
tickets: 650.725.ARTS * www.ticketweb.com

Latin Music Books & CDs from Sher Music Co

The Latin Real Book (C, Bb or Eb)

The only professional-level Latin fake book ever published! Over 570 pages. Includes detailed transcriptions of tunes, exactly as recorded by:

Ray Barretto
Eddie Palmieri
Fania All-Stars
Tito Puente
Ruben Blades
Los Van Van
NG La Banda

Irakere
Celia Cruz
Arsenio Rodriguez
Tito Rodriguez
Orquesta Aragon
Beny Moré
Cal Tjader

Andy Narell
Mario Bauza
Dizzy Gilllespie
Mongo Santamaria
Manny Oquendo & Libre
Puerto Rico All-Stars
Issac Delgaldo

Ft. Apache Band
Dave Valentin
Paquito D'Rivera
Clare Fischer
Chick Corea
Sergio Mendes
Ivan Lins

Djavan
Tom Jobim
Toninho Horta
Joao Bosco
Milton Nascimento
Leila Pinheiro
Gal Costa
And Many More!

Muy Caliente!

Afro-Cuban Play-Along CD and Book
Rebeca Mauleón - Keyboard
Oscar Stagnaro - Bass
Orestes Vilató - Timbales
Carlos Caro - Bongos
Edgardo Cambon - Congas
Over 70 min. of smokin' Latin grooves!
Stereo separation so you can eliminate the bass or piano. Play-along with a rhythm section featuring some of the top Afro-Cuban musicians in the world!

The Latin Real Book Sampler CD

12 of the greatest Latin Real Book tunes as played by the original artists: Tito Puente, Ray Barretto, Andy Narell, Puerto Rico Allstars, Bacacoto, etc.

$16 list price. Available in U.S.A. only.

101 Montunos

by Rebeca Mauleón

The only comprehensive study of Latin piano playing ever published.

- Bi-lingual text (English/Spanish)
- 2 CDs of the author demonstrating each montuno
- Covers over 100 years of Afro-Cuban styles, including the danzón, guaracha, mambo, merengue and songo—from Peruchin to Eddie Palmieri.

The True Cuban Bass

By Carlos Del Puerto, (bassist with Irakere) and **Silvio Vergara**, $22.

For acoustic or electric bass; English and Spanish text; Includes CDs of either historic Cuban recordings or Carlos playing each exercise; Many transcriptions of complete bass parts for tunes in different Cuban styles – the roots of Salsa.

The Brazilian Guitar Book

by **Nelson Faria**, one of Brazil's best new guitarists.

- Over 140 pages of comping patterns, transcriptions and chord melodies for samba, bossa, baiaõ, etc.
- Complete chord voicings written out for each example.
- Comes with a CD of Nelson playing each example.
- The most complete Brazilian guitar method ever published! $28 list price.

Joe Diorio – "Nelson Faria's book is a welcome addition to the guitar literature. I'm sure those who work with this volume will benefit greatly"

The Salsa Guide Book

By Rebeca Mauleón

The only complete method book on salsa ever published! 260 pages. $25

Carlos Santana – "A true treasure of knowledge and information about Afro-Cuban music."
Mark Levine, author of The Jazz Piano Book. – "This is the book on salsa."
Sonny Bravo, pianist with Tito Puente – "This will be the salsa 'bible' for years to come."
Oscar Hernández, pianist with Rubén Blades – "An excellent and much needed resource."

The New Real Book Series

The Standards Real Book (C, Bb or Eb)

Alice In Wonderland
All Of You
Alone Together
At Last
Baltimore Oriole
A Beautiful Friendship
Bess, You Is My Woman
But Not For Me
Close Enough For Love
Crazy He Calls Me
Dancing In The Dark
Days Of Wine And Roses
Dreamsville
Easy To Love
Embraceable You

Falling In Love With Love
From This Moment On
Give Me The Simple Life
Have You Met Miss Jones?
Hey There
I Can't Get Started
I Concentrate On You
I Cover The Waterfront
I Love You
I Loves You Porgy
I Only Have Eyes For You
I Wish I Knew
I'm A Fool To Want You
Indian Summer
It Ain't Necessarily So

It Never Entered My Mind
It's You Or No One
Just One Of Those Things
Love For Sale
Love Walked In
Lover, Come Back To Me
The Man I Love
Mr. Lucky
My Funny Valentine
My Heart Stood Still
My Man's Gone Now
Old Folks
On A Clear Day
Our Love Is Here To Stay
Secret Love

September In The Rain
Serenade In Blue
Shiny Stockings
Since I Fell For You
So In Love
So Nice (Summer Samba)
Some Other Time
Stormy Weather
The Summer Knows
Summer Night
Summertime
Teach Me Tonight
That Sunday, That Summer
Then I'll Be Tired Of You
There's No You

A Time For Love
Time On My Hands
'Tis Autumn
Where Or When
Who Cares?
With A Song In My Heart
You Go To My Head
Ain't No Sunshine
'Round Midnight
The Girl From Ipanema
Bluesette
And Hundreds More!

The New Real Book - Volume 1 (C, Bb or Eb)

Angel Eyes
Anthropology
Autumn Leaves
Beautiful Love
Bernie's Tune
Blue Bossa
Blue Daniel
But Beautiful
Chain Of Fools
Chelsea Bridge
Compared To What
Darn That Dream
Desafinado
Early Autumn
Eighty One

E.S.P.
Everything Happens To Me
Fall
Feel Like Makin' Love
Footprints
Four
Four On Six
Gee Baby Ain't I Good
To You
Gone With The Wind
Here's That Rainy Day
I Love Lucy
I Mean You
I Should Care
I Thought About You

If I Were A Bell
Imagination
The Island
Jersey Bounce
Joshua
Lady Bird
Like Someone In Love
Line For Lyons
Little Sunflower
Lush Life
Mercy, Mercy, Mercy
The Midnight Sun
Monk's Mood
Moonlight In Vermont
My Shining Hour

Nature Boy
Nefertiti
Nothing Personal
Oleo
Once I Loved
Out Of This World
Pent Up House
Polkadots And Moon-
beams
Portrait Of Tracy
Put It Where You Want It
Robbin's Nest
Ruby, My Dear
Satin Doll
Search For Peace

Shaker Song
Skylark
A Sleepin' Bee
Solar
Speak No Evil
St. Thomas
Street Life
Tenderly
These Foolish Things
This Masquerade
Three Views Of A Secret
Waltz For Debby
Willow Weep For Me
And Many More!

The New Real Book - Volume 2 (C, Bb or Eb)

Afro-Centric
After You've Gone
Along Came Betty
Bessie's Blues
Black Coffee
Blues For Alice
Body And Soul
Bolivia
The Boy Next Door
Bye Bye Blackbird
Cherokee
A Child Is Born
Cold Duck Time
Day By Day

Django
Equinox
Exactly Like You
Falling Grace
Five Hundred Miles High
Freedom Jazz Dance
Giant Steps
Got A Match?
Harlem Nocturne
Hi-Fly
Honeysuckle Rose
I Hadn't Anyone 'Til You
I'll Be Around
I'll Get By

Ill Wind
I'm Glad There Is You
Impressions
In Your Own Sweet Way
It's The Talk Of The Town
Jordu
Killer Joe
Lullaby Of The Leaves
Manha De Carnaval
The Masquerade Is Over
Memories Of You
Moment's Notice
Mood Indigo
My Ship

Naima
Nica's Dream
Once In A While
Perdido
Rosetta
Sea Journey
Senor Blues
September Song
Seven Steps To Heaven
Silver's Serenade
So Many Stars
Some Other Blues
Song For My Father
Sophisticated Lady

Spain
Stablemates
Stardust
Sweet And Lovely
That's All
There Is No Greater Love
'Til There Was You
Time Remembered
Turn Out The Stars
Unforgettable
While We're Young
Whisper Not
Will You Still Be Mine?
You're Everything
And Many More!

The New Real Book - Volume 3 (C, Bb, Eb or Bass clef)

Actual Proof
Ain't That Peculair
Almost Like Being In Love
Another Star
Autumn Serenade
Bird Of Beauty
Black Nile
Blue Moon
Butterfly
Caravan
Ceora
Close Your Eyes
Creepin'
Day Dream
Dolphin Dance

Don't Be That Way
Don't Blame Me
Emily
Everything I Have Is
Yours
For All We Know
Freedomland
The Gentle Rain
Get Ready
A Ghost Of A Chance
Heat Wave
How Sweet It Is
I Fall In Love Too Easily
I Got It Bad

I Hear A Rhapsody
If You Could See Me Now
In A Mellow Tone
In A Sentimental Mood
Inner Urge
Invitation
The Jitterbug Waltz
Just Friends
Just You, Just Me
Knock On Wood
The Lamp Is Low
Laura
Let's Stay Together
Litha
Lonely Woman

Maiden Voyage
Moon And Sand
Moonglow
My Girl
On Green Dolphin Street
Over The Rainbow
Prelude To A Kiss
Respect
Ruby
The Second Time Around
Serenata
The Shadow Of Your Smile
So Near, So Far
Solitude
Speak Like A Child
Spring Is Here

Stairway To The Stars
Star Eyes
Stars Fell On Alabama
Stompin' At The Savoy
Sugar
Sweet Lorraine
Taking A Chance On Love
This Is New
Too High
(Used To Be A) Cha Cha
When Lights Are Low
You Must Believe In Spring
And Many More!

Other Jazz Publications

The Jazz Theory Book

By Mark Levine, the most comprehensive Jazz Theory book ever published! $38 list price.

- Over 500 pages of text and over 750 musical examples.
- Written in the language of the working jazz musician, this book is easy to read and user-friendly. At the same time, it is the most comprehensive study of jazz harmony and theory ever published.
- Mark Levine has worked with Bobby Hutcherson, Cal Tjader, Joe Henderson, Woody Shaw, and many other jazz greats.

The European Real Book

An amazing collection of some of the greatest jazz compositions ever recorded! Available in C, Bb and Eb. $40

- Over 100 of Europe's best jazz writers.
- 100% accurate, composer-approved charts.
- 400 pages of fresh, exciting sounds from virtually every country in Europe.
- Sher Music's superior legibility and signature calligraphy makes reading the music easy.

Listen to FREE MP3 FILES of many of the songs at www.shermusic.com!

The Jazz Piano Book

By Mark Levine, Concord recording artist and pianist with Cal Tjader. For beginning to advanced pianists. The only truly comprehensive method ever published! Over 300 pages. $32

Richie Beirach –"The best new method book available."
Hal Galper – "This is a must!"
Jamey Aebersold – "This is an invaluable resource for any pianist."
James Williams – "One of the most complete anthologies on jazz piano."

Also available in Spanish! ¡El Libro del Jazz Piano!

Concepts For Bass Soloing

By Chuck Sher and Marc Johnson, (bassist with Bill Evans, etc.) The only book ever published that is specifically designed to improve your soloing! $26

- Includes two CDs of Marc Johnson soloing on each exercise
- Transcriptions of bass solos by: Eddie Gomez, John Patitucci, Scott LaFaro, Jimmy Haslip, etc.

"It's a pleasure to encounter a Bass Method so well conceived and executed." – **Steve Swallow**

The Yellowjackets Songbook

Complete package contains six separate spiral-bound books, one each for:
- Piano/partial score • C melody lead sheet
- Synthesizer/miscellaneous parts
- Bb & Eb Horn melody part • Bass • Drums

Contains 20 great tunes from their entire career.
Charts exactly as recorded – approved by the Yellowjackets. World famous Sher Music Co. accuracy and legibility. Over 400 pages, $38 list price.

The Improvisor's Bass Method

By Chuck Sher. A complete method for electric or acoustic bass, plus transcribed solos and bass lines by Mingus, Jaco, Ron Carter, Scott LaFaro, Paul Jackson, Ray Brown, and more! Over 200 pages. $16

International Society of Bassists – "Undoubtedly the finest book of its kind."
Eddie Gomez – "Informative, readily comprehensible and highly imaginative"

The World's Greatest Fake Book

Jazz & Fusion Tunes by: **Coltrane, Mingus, Jaco, Chick Corea, Bird, Herbie Hancock, Bill Evans, McCoy, Beirach, Ornette, Wayne Shorter, Zawinul, AND MANY MORE!** $32

Chick Corea – "Great for any students of jazz.'
Dave Liebman – "The fake book of the 80's."
George Cables – "The most carefully conceived fake book I've ever seen."

The Jazz Solos of Chick Corea

Over 150 pages of Chick's greatest solos; "Spain", "Litha", "Windows", "Sicily", etc. for all instrumentalists, single line transcriptions, not full piano score. $18

Chick Corea – "I don't know anyone I would trust more to correctly transcribe my improvisations."

The New Real Book Play-Along CDs (For Volume 1)

CD #1 - Jazz Classics - Lady Bird, Bouncin' With Bud, Up Jumped Spring, Monk's Mood, Doors, Very Early, Eighty One, Voyage **& More!**
CD #2 - Choice Standards - Beautiful Love, Darn That Dream, Moonlight In Vermont, Trieste, My Shining Hour, I Should Care **& More!**
CD #3 - Pop-Fusion - Morning Dance, Nothing Personal, La Samba, Hideaway, This Masquerade, Three Views Of A Secret, Rio **& More!**
World-Class Rhythm Sections, featuring Mark Levine, Larry Dunlap, Sky Evergreen, Bob Magnusson, Keith Jones, Vince Lateano & Tom Hayashi

Recent Sher Music Publications

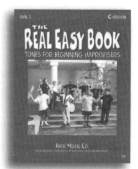

The Real Easy Book Vol. 1
TUNES FOR BEGINNING IMPROVISERS

Published by Sher Music Co. in conjunction with the Stanford Jazz Workshop. $19 list price.

The easiest tunes from Horace Silver, Eddie Harris, Freddie Hubbard, Red Garland, Sonny Rollins, Cedar Walton, Wes Montgomery Cannonball Adderly, etc. Get yourself or your beginning jazz combo sounding good right away with the first fake book ever designed for the beginning improviser.
Available in C, Bb, Eb and Bass Clef.

The Real Easy Book Vol. 2
TUNES FOR INTERMEDIATE IMPROVISERS

Published by Sher Music Co. in conjunction with the Stanford Jazz Workshop. Over 240 pages. $29.

The best intermediate-level tunes by: Charlie Parker, John Coltrane, Miles Davis, John Scofield, Sonny Rollins, Horace Silver, Wes Montgomery, Freddie Hubbard, Cal Tjader, Cannonball Adderly, and more!
Both volumes feature instructional material tailored for each tune. Perfect for jazz combos!
Available in C, Bb, Eb and Bass Clef.

The All Jazz Real Book

Over 540 pages of tunes as recorded by: Miles, Trane, Bill Evans, Cannonball, Scofield, Brecker, Yellowjackets, Bird, Mulgrew Miller, Kenny Werner, MJQ, McCoy Tyner, Kurt Elling, Brad Mehldau, Don Grolnick, Kenny Garrett, Patitucci, Jerry Bergonzi, Stanley Clarke, Tom Harrell, Herbie Hancock, Horace Silver, Stan Getz, Sonny Rollins, and MORE!

Includes a free CD of many of the melodies (featuring Bob Sheppard & Friends.). $44 list price.
Available in C, Bb, Eb

The Latin Bass Book
A PRACTICAL GUIDE
By Oscar Stagnaro

The only comprehensive book ever published on how to play bass in authentic Afro-Cuban, Brazilian, Caribbean, Latin Jazz & South American styles.
$34 list price

Over 250 pages of transcriptions of Oscar Stagnaro playing each exercise. Learn from the best!

Includes: 3 Play-Along CDs to accompany each exercise, featuring world-class rhythm sections.

Metaphors For The Musician
By Randy Halberstadt

This practical and enlightening book will help any jazz player or vocalist look at music with "new eyes." Designed for any level of player, on any instrument, "Metaphors For The Musician" provides numerous exercises throughout to help the reader turn these concepts into musical reality.

Guaranteed to help you improve your musicianship. 330 pages - $29 list price. Satisfaction guaranteed!

Inside The Brazilian Rhythm Section
By Nelson Faria and Cliff Korman

This is the first book/CD package ever published that provides an opportunity for bassists, guitarists, pianists and drummers to interact and play-along with a master Brazilian rhythm section. Perfect for practicing both accompanying and soloing.

$28 list price for book and 2 CDs - including the charts for the CD tracks and sample parts for each instrument, transcribed from the recording. Satisfaction guaranteed!

The finest in Jazz & Latin publications
SHER MUSIC CO.
www.shermusic.com

See **www.shermusic.com** for more information, including a complete list of tunes in all our fake books.
To order, call (800) 444-7437 or fax (707) 763-2038